THEN & NOW

VISALIA

Opposite: On September 2, 1914, Harry Graeter opened his new confectionery shop at the corner of Main and Court Streets. He spared no expense on furnishings and decorations, spending about $22,000 to make it a showplace. The "Palace of Sweets" had wall murals, French-beveled mirrors and beautiful marble, and was reported to be the finest of its kind between San Francisco and Los Angeles. Even though it was known for its delicious ice cream and candy, breakfast, lunch, and dinner were also served at Graeter's along with afternoon tea.

THEN & NOW

VISALIA

Terry L. Ommen

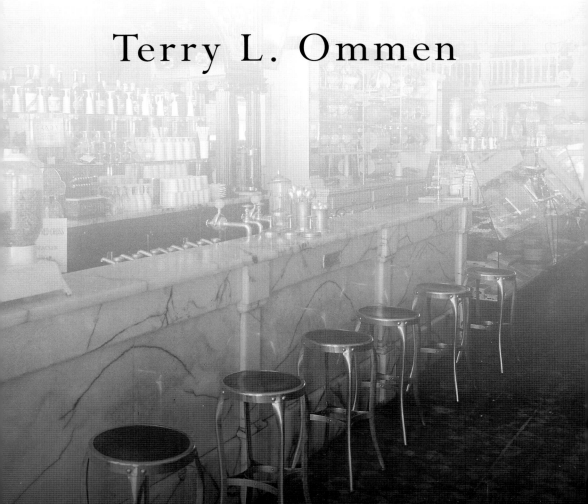

Library of Congress control number: 2008940178

Published by Arcadia Publishing
Charleston SC, Chicago IL, Portsmouth NH, San Francisco CA

Printed in the United States of America

For all general information contact Arcadia Publishing at:
Telephone 843-853-2070
Fax 843-853-0044
E-mail sales@arcadiapublishing.com
For customer service and orders:
Toll-Free 1-888-313-2665

Visit us on the Internet at www.arcadiapublishing.com

This book is dedicated to all those who lived our history and to all those who took the time to record it for us to enjoy.

ON THE FRONT COVER: The statue of "Soldier at Parade Rest" was placed at the Visalia Cemetery by the local chapter of the Grand Army of the Republic in 1916. (Courtesy Visalia Public Cemetery District.)

ON THE BACK COVER: An unidentified man in a roadster poses on West Main Street around 1915.

Contents

ACKNOWLEDGMENTS

In 1865, Lewis Carroll wrote in his book *Alice's Adventures in Wonderland*, "What is the use of a book without pictures or conversations?" Pictures give us a visual understanding and help us interpret the words. Obviously any photographic history book such as this relies heavily on old photographs with accurate documentation. Much credit for this book needs to go to the many early photographers and historians, oftentimes unidentified, from whom we have inherited a great collection of photographs.

In addition, there are other guardians of our photographic record who unselfishly shared their collection for this history book. To Marian Cote, Sharon Doughty, Laura Heberling, Russ Hurley, Guy Shelley, and Ida Thut, I am very grateful. Thanks also to Rob Speidel, who, with the blessing of his mother, Kathryn Speidel Crookshanks, shared the collection of photographs from his father, the late Robert M. Speidel.

Historical organizations also contributed generously. The Annie R. Mitchell History Room at the Tulare County Library in Visalia provided images in this book and other valuable reference material. To Dona Shores, district manager of the Visalia Public Cemetery District, who kindly shared the vintage photograph shown on the cover, I especially want to thank you. Kathy McGowan, curator of the Tulare County Museum at Mooney Grove Park, shared photographs and reference material from the collection, and her help was invaluable. As a result, proceeds from the sale of this book will be donated to the Tulare County Historical Society to be used for improvement projects at the museum.

Alan George and Joseph Vicenti, both local historians, were important resources in completing this book. Their careful review of the photographs and documentation provided much needed validation, and this book is improved because of their involvement.

John Poultney of Arcadia Publishing deserves special thanks. He was always helpful and provided much needed encouragement throughout the project. Working with John was a pleasure.

Finally, my wife, Laraine, has shared this project with me from the beginning. She has been my scheduler, proofreader, editor, critic, and supporter, and without her willingness to be a partner, I would not have accepted this project. To her I owe much, and for our shared love I am very grateful.

INTRODUCTION

Visalia is the oldest town in California's San Joaquin Valley, between Stockton and Los Angeles. The town began on the north bank of Mill Creek in 1852 in the middle of a large oak forest in an area then known as "Four Creeks Country." Visalia was situated in the beautiful Kaweah River Delta region. The soil was rich, water was plentiful, and the Valley Oak trees provided lumber and shade. Today many of these magnificent trees are gone, but those remaining are protected by local ordinance.

The first settlers were fearful of the local Native Americans living nearby, so they built a log fort for protection. Experiencing no hostile treatment, the settlers soon abandoned the fort and started building the town.

One of the settlers was Nathaniel Vise, an adventurous nomadic man who had come to this area from Visalia, Kentucky, a town named for his family. Vise had laid claim to a considerable amount of land around the fort but surrendered it, and soon thereafter in his honor, the town became known as Visalia.

In 1853, Visalia became the county seat of Tulare County and has been ever since. In the 1850s and 1860s, it served as a mining supply town for the Kern River mines and the "diggings" east of the Sierra Nevada range in the Owens Valley region. The Butterfield Overland Mail Company came through Visalia in 1858 and made it a regular stage stop on the route. In 1859, Visalia established the first newspaper in the southern San Joaquin Valley, called the *Tulare County Record and Fresno Examiner*, and in 1860 the town saw the telegraph arrive. During the Civil War years, the town gained notoriety as a haven for Southern sympathizers and as a result became embroiled in Civil War politics and violence.

The decades that followed brought the good and the bad. Railroads came in, and criminals soon arrived, bringing with them a period of lawlessness. Much needed and appreciated electricity came thanks to the Mount Whitney Power Company's hydroelectric efforts on the Kaweah River.

As the 20th century arrived, the town's population had grown to about 3,000. The citizens had experienced much up to that point—some good, some bad, but more challenges were coming. The arrival of the automobile, the banning of alcohol, the influenza epidemic, devastating fires, and numerous floods were all confronted. Despite the difficulties, the town continued to grow and prosper. In 1930, the population was about 7,200, by 1950 about 12,000, and by the year 2000, the population had reached almost 92,000.

In 2008, approximately 122,000 people called Visalia home. Despite its relatively large population, the town has been able to maintain a small-town "feel." The downtown business district is thriving, and business leaders have found the secret for maintaining a vibrant downtown core.

Part of that prosperity undoubtedly is the result of Visalians realizing that preserving old buildings and converting them to contemporary uses makes good business sense, and today many of our old buildings have been restored and are being used. After 156 years, the city of Visalia remains the "Queen of the San Joaquin."

STATELY STATUES AND DELIGHTFUL DIVERSIONS

In 1916, the local chapter of the Grand Army of the Republic (GAR) and its auxiliary, the Woman's Relief Corps (WRC), placed a statue of "Soldier at Parade Rest" at the Visalia Cemetery, in the Civil War section. Made of molded sheets of bronze by the W. H. Mullins Company, the monument was dedicated on Memorial Day, May 30, 1916, paying tribute to Civil War soldiers. Today the monument continues to stand, although it is beginning to show its age.

From 1912 to 1917, road races were held on city streets. These races were immensely popular and attracted thousands of race fans who lined the streets to watch the action. The photograph below shows an unidentified race car driver and his mechanic posing near 116 West Main Street. These buildings remain today and are located in the core of the downtown district. The person in the front row, third from the left, is Alvin Shippey. No one else is positively identified.

Before each annual rodeo, Visalia had a rodeo parade. In June 1938, this entry was decorated by the local Veterans of Foreign Wars (VFW) Auxiliary for the parade and won first prize for best decorated car. Shown on Main Street with the Fox Theatre in the background, the winning car has children riding on the fenders and hood. They are, from left to right, Charlene Sharp, Francis Bufkin, and Wanda Sharp.

James Earle Fraser sculpted the *End of the Trail* statue for San Francisco's 1915 Panama Pacific International Exposition. In 1919, Tulare County purchased it and placed it in Mooney Grove Park. In 1968, the National Cowboy and Western Heritage Museum in Oklahoma City offered to trade the original statue for a bronze replica. The county agreed and the replica stands today at Mooney Grove Park. The restored original proudly greets visitors entering the Oklahoma City museum.

American sculptor Solon Borglum created *The Pioneer, A Reverie* for San Francisco's 1915 Panama Pacific International Exposition. Made of plaster, it stood 20 feet high and represented an early pioneer on horseback. After the exposition, the sculpture was acquired by Tulare County for Visalia's Mooney Grove Park and in 1916 was placed near the park entrance. In 1980, weakened from age, the statue totally collapsed, breaking into many pieces. Only the pedestal remains today.

Members of the Visalia Kiwanis Club pose with Col. John R. White, superintendent of Sequoia National Park. Standing near the east entrance to the Jacob Building on Church Street, just south of Main Street, in this 1938 photograph are, from left to right, Dickson Maddox, Kiwanis president Arch Nichols, Col. John White, and Roy Brooks. The granite trim on this 1894 building was quarried in the foothills east of Exeter, California. The building continues to be used for retail and office space.

STATELY STATUES AND DELIGHTFUL DIVERSIONS

An Entrance to Visalia, Cal.

In the 1920s, the west entrance into Visalia was on Main Street. The Dudley House stood at Giddings Avenue, adjacent to a native Valley Oak tree that grew in the intersection. The city created an 8-foot, 9.5-inch by 6-foot, 7-inch area that was designated Lone Oak Park. It was known as the smallest park in the world until 1936 when the tree was deemed a traffic hazard and cut down, and thus the park was gone.

In 1919, John Cutler Jr. donated a heavily wooded 70-acre parcel to the County of Tulare for a park. Located adjacent to the St. Johns River on Houston Avenue, the park was named in honor of the donor's father, John Cutler, an 1852 pioneer of Tulare County. The senior Cutler was a big farmer and one of Tulare County's first judges. Cutler Park continues to provide recreational opportunities under the shade of a beautiful forest of Valley Oak trees.

In 1927, the Western Auto Supply Company and the *Visalia Times Delta* newspaper sponsored an electronic scoreboard for the World Series. The scoreboard was against the east exterior wall of the California Hotel. As the games between the New York Yankees and the Pittsburgh Pirates were broadcast by radio, the crowd on Bridge Street watched the staff make the scoreboard changes. The hotel at the northeast corner of Bridge and Main Streets is gone, replaced by a parking lot.

In 1910, surveyor George D. Smith presented a plat map to the Visalia City Council showing what was to become Highland Park. Located in the Highland Tract on Highland Avenue, this island park, approximately 30 feet by 71 feet in size, was built to protect the oak trees inside. In 1914, the manual training students from Visalia High School placed a concrete marker in the park. The park and the concrete marker remain today.

STATELY STATUES AND DELIGHTFUL DIVERSIONS

POUNDING
THE PAVEMENT

Aviation cadets assigned to the Visalia-Dinuba School of Aeronautics at Sequoia Field marched on Main Street near Encina Street during a parade in July 1944. The cadets were training to become military pilots and Sequoia Field, located a few miles north of Visalia, offered them plenty of open space for practice. The buildings on this section of West Main Street continue to look much like they did in 1944.

About 1907, a Visalia street crew is shown working on Church Street between Acequia and Main Streets. Working by hand with picks, they break up old asphalt material and prepare to resurface the street. The Old Palm Garden Saloon was a popular hangout, and a little further down the street on the right is the Gray Horse Harness Shop with its recognizable horse statue on the roof. It continues to be a popular retail area.

In 1910, Mill Creek, which flows through the city, was lined with cement and covered. Roads and buildings were constructed over it and about one-third of a mile of Mill Creek flows below the surface today. The lining and covering of Mill Creek was predicted by some to be the answer to the flooding problem, but unfortunately flooding continued. This photograph shows the lining and covering work being done on Mill Creek below Center Street between Court and Church Streets.

In the 1950s, on the southeast corner of Court and Center Streets, stood a number of retail businesses and buildings, all of which are now gone to make way for parking lots. The two-story wooden structure on the right was constructed in 1886 as the Palace Hotel annex building, which served as an extension of the hotel. Even though virtually all the structures shown are gone, the old Bank of Italy building in the background remains.

In 1930, the Fox Theatre was built at what was considered the western edge of downtown. It was said the theater tower stood "high in the air like a lighthouse above a seaport," anchoring the west end of Main Street. However, in the late 1940s, the downtown expanded and this area near Floral and Main Streets flourished with national chain stores and local independent businesses. The Fox clock tower has become the logo for the downtown business district.

Taken in 1863, this is one of the oldest known photographs of Visalia. Looking east from the intersection of Court and Main Streets, wagons can be seen unattended. Also, on the right near the center of the photograph is a hand pump and water trough that provided water to thirsty teams of horses. Retail businesses lined both sides of Main Street, and it continues to be the heart of the downtown business district today.

The north side of Main Street between Locust and Court Streets shows relics of the past. Parking meters and the old ornate streetlights no longer exist, and the 1950s-era businesses are gone, but the buildings remain. Main Drug, a landmark at Main and Locust Streets, was opened around 1934 by W. C. "Doby" Lovelace. In 1968, the Mar family purchased the drugstore and owned it until 1999. Now new businesses occupy the buildings.

Located at 221 West Main Street, the Palace Stable was owned and operated by Missouri native William R. Bowen, shown on the left in this *c.* 1905 photograph. The livery stable provided board and care for horses and rental services for buggies. Bowen was known as a man who knew how to care for and treat animals, an important skill for someone in the livery business. This site is now in the center of a growing downtown retail center.

In the 1960s, the downtown district contained many small businesses in older buildings. Parking was limited primarily to the street, with very little off-street parking available. During this time, revitalization moved forward, and many of the old structures were demolished to make way for new ones with more parking. These buildings, located on the north side of the street in the 200 block of East Main Street, are gone now and a large business parking lot has taken their place.

Made of redwood, this building was constructed in 1873 on the northeast corner of Church and Center Streets. It was a joint construction project between the local Masons and the Odd Fellows and became the meeting hall for both. Eventually the building was sold to Tulare County, and it was demolished in 1963; however, part of the front facade was saved and continues to be part of the Tulare County Museum at Mooney Grove Park.

In 1902, there were four automobiles in Tulare County, but it did not take long for these horseless carriages to become popular. By the 1920s, the county had many dealerships, including Visalia's Willimott Motor Company, a Chevrolet dealer located at 219 West Main Street. Obviously happy with the new automobiles, the dealership proudly displayed them on Main Street. The building was used as auto garages over the years, but it now houses restaurants and shops.

The Moore's Auto Stage Company had its office in the Hotel Johnson building in the 200 block of East Main Street. Tours to Sequoia National Park were organized from here using these Packard automobile stages. John E. Moore operated the touring company into the 1920s. The Hotel Johnson building was damaged beyond repair by fire in 1968 and was demolished. A bank now occupies the site of the Hotel Johnson.

On the right side of this 1908 photograph is the Santa Fe Railroad depot and behind it the Visalia Milling Company. The mill is on an original mill site dating back to 1853; a medical office now occupies the space. The depot, on the southwest corner of Main Street and Santa Fe Avenue, was built shortly after the Santa Fe Railroad took over operations in 1900. The depot was torn down about 1968, and now a restaurant is located there.

This 1920-licensed GMC truck with two trailers is shown making a wide turn from Bridge Street onto Center Street in Chinatown. The vehicle, loaded with concrete pipe, can be seen passing a number of Chinese and Japanese businesses. The buildings on the left, or north side of Center Street, no longer are standing. However, the brick building on the right, believed to have been constructed in 1894, remains today and houses restaurants.

The Visalia Cooperative Creamery building was constructed in 1910 on the north side of Oak Street, between Church and Garden Streets. Constructed as a state-of-the-art creamery, the brick structure cost about $18,000 to build, which included the equipment inside. When the creamery started production, it manufactured about 400 pounds of butter per day. The Visalia Electric Railroad lines can be seen overhead. The building now houses an art studio.

Jacob V. Huffaker started his livery stable business around 1870. Located on the northwest corner of Court and Acequia Streets, the Overland Livery Stable was considered Visalia's oldest stable for many years. Huffaker sold the business, and a fire severely damaged the old wooden structure in 1916. Repair was considered, but it was deemed a firetrap and torn down. Today the site provides valuable parking spaces for a thriving downtown.

WADING OUT THE WATER

During the 1955–1956 winter season, excessive rain left many of the streets flooded. A logjam in the Mill Creek channel, which flows under downtown, caused it to overflow its banks, resulting in severe damage to homes and businesses. In this view, looking north on Church Street from Main Street, sandbags can be seen, but they did very little to stop the water damage. Redevelopment efforts removed many of these buildings, and parking lots have replaced them.

The flood of 1906 filled the streets of Visalia with water. This view, looking east on Main Street from Church Street, shows floodwaters approaching businesses on both sides of Main Street. On the left, the water is about to go over the sidewalk into the Visalia House, and on the right, the Gray Horse Harness Shop is about to flood as well. The Visalia House was torn down in 1916, and the harness shop was torn down in 1941.

WADING OUT THE WATER

For almost 80 years, Visalia's fabulous Fox Theatre has stood as a landmark at Main and Encina Streets. The grand opening was celebrated on February 27, 1930, to a full house, all cheering for the Zane Grey western *Lone Star Ranger*. In 1999, the old movie house was restored to its originally beauty, reopened, and continues to be a very recognizable icon representing the historic downtown district. It has withstood considerable adversity, including the difficult February 1945 flood.

Before the Terminus Dam and Reservoir was completed in 1962, Visalia flooded frequently. The 1955 flood was especially destructive as Mill Creek, which flows under the city, became clogged and overflowed. Despite widespread damage, Visalians kept their sense of humor. The Visalia Theatre marquee in the distance reads, "Alan Ladd—Hell on Visalia Bay," a spoof on the famous actor's movie *Hell on Frisco Bay*. Sandbags could not contain the floodwaters on Garden Street near Main Street.

WADING OUT THE WATER

In 1937, the Purity Stores chain opened a new Visalia grocery store on the northeast corner of Locust and Center Streets. Thoroughly modern and complete with a full line of groceries, including fruit, vegetable, and meat departments, the store proudly boasted attractive display cases throughout. The disastrous flood of 1945 took its toll on the downtown district, and the Purity Store became a victim. Today the building at 120 West Center Street is a title company.

In 1890, the two-story Tulare County Jail was built on the northeast corner of Oak and Church Streets. Made of brick with granite trim in an Italian style, it was touted as being "architecturally perfect." However, it did not hold Grat Dalton, of the famous Dalton Gang, who escaped from this jail in 1891. Shown here during the 1906 flood, the building was demolished in 1918 and a new Tulare County jail was built on the exact site. It houses a restaurant and offices today.

During the flood of 1955–1956, merchants tried desperately to protect their property. Despite valiant efforts, many business owners and home owners suffered severe losses as water entered into their buildings. When floodwaters subsided, they faced huge cleanup efforts. More than 40,000 sandbags were used to control the raging water. This photograph was taken looking north in front of Sponsler's Floral Shop at 117 North Encina Street, now a furniture store.

A National Guard soldier stands watch on Court Street at Oak Street during the major flood of 1955–1956. The Tulare County Courthouse annex building is on the left and the downtown business district is in the distance in this photograph looking south on Court Street. The Hotel Johnson catering truck was probably involved in relief or cleanup efforts. About 72 blocks were under water for five days.

In 1945, a break in the levee on the nearby St. Johns River caused a disastrous flood to hit downtown. The center of town, Court and Main Streets, is shown here with flooded businesses on the south side of Main Street, between Court and Church Streets. Damage was excessive, and the call for a dam to be constructed to control mountain runoff was heard again. It took until 1962 to complete Terminus Dam.

The flood of 1906 not only created problems for pedestrians and buggies, it also made it difficult for trains. This photograph, taken from Courthouse Square looking northwest through the intersection of Court and Oak Streets, shows a Southern Pacific locomotive slowly traveling westbound on Oak Street through flooded tracks. Although the houses in the background are gone, the decorative granite curbing around Courthouse Square continues to be in place.

CHAPTER 4

STRICTLY BUSINESS

In 1916, the brick building at the corner of Locust and Center Streets was constructed as the Studebaker automobile dealership. Homer Patterson was the dealer and his business was prosperous at "Studebaker Corner." About 1930, the dealership moved, and over the years the building became home to various auto repair businesses, retail stores, and nightclubs. In 2004, the building was purchased by the First Presbyterian Church, completely restored, and is now a youth and community center.

The S. Sweet Company operated from 1857 to 1931. For years, the store stood on the south side of the 100 block of East Main Street. This 1890 photograph shows the following men next to the curb from left to right: Dr. Hall, William Hammond, Henry Jerusalem, George Butz, Leon Goldstein, Fred Williams, and Theodore Loventhal. Note the team tied to a hitching ring, several of which can still be found in the curbs. These buildings no longer exist, but shops continue to line the street.

The Hotel American building was constructed in the early 1900s on the northwest corner of Main and Garden Streets. There was quite a stir in 1914 when the hotel proprietor was arrested for illegally selling alcohol, which was known as "blind pigging." Later the building became the Travelers Hotel. In the late 1960s, it fell victim to urban renewal and was demolished. Today the site is a parking lot.

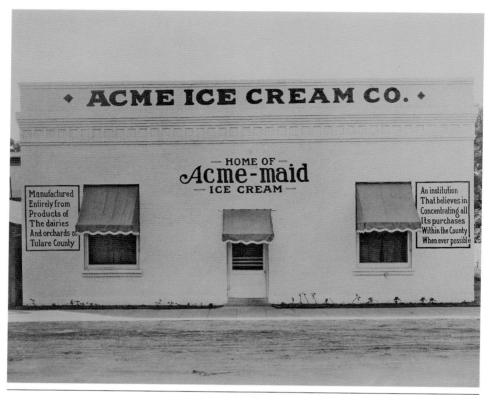

The Acme Ice Cream Company made ice cream in this building and won a gold medal at the California and Southwestern States Ice Cream Manufacturer's Association Convention in Stockton, California, in 1921. The company later became the Valley Ice Cream Company. In the 1950s, the building became a paint shop. Today this 1912 vintage structure at 307 North Garden Street is home to an insurance agency.

The Old Drug House building was constructed about 1857 on the southwest corner of Main and Church Streets. Around 1860, Elias Jacob purchased it, and the second story became home to the first Masonic temple in Visalia. In 1894, the Casino Saloon on the ground floor caught fire, and the building burned beyond repair. That same year, Elias Jacob constructed a new building on the same site, which is still in use today as a retail and office space.

David Chan and his brother Gay started as vegetable peddlers in Visalia, but as business grew, they placed a small tin shack at 115 North Locust Street and continued to sell produce. About 1937, they built a market on the site that was to become Chan Brothers Market. The grocery store was a popular business and operated as Chan's Market until the late 1960s. Many retail businesses have occupied the building since the market closed.

STRICTLY BUSINESS

Businessman Herbert Askin operated his plumbing and tinning business at 219 West Main Street from about 1904 to 1911. He was forced to move by a superior court judge who lived nearby and objected to the noise. Askin served as a city trustee (city council member) from 1907 until 1919, the last four years as president (mayor). Askin may be in this *c.* 1905 photograph, but it cannot be verified. Today retail businesses surround the area.

Construction of the Hotel Johnson was completed in 1917. Known as the "Queen Hotel of the Valley," the $150,000, five-story building, located on the corner of Church and Main Streets, was the pride of Visalia. In 1968, it caught fire and was damaged beyond repair. Two people were killed. The remains of the hotel were removed, and for a number of years the lot was vacant. A bank was built on the site in the mid-1970s.

The Mount Whitney Power and Electric Company was incorporated in 1899. Its office was on Court Street initially, and in 1912 the company constructed this building. Trewhitt and Shields of Hanford built it at a cost of $30,000. In 1920, Mount Whitney Power was sold to Southern California Edison. The building, located at 213 West Main Street, has been modified considerably over the years and now contains retail shops.

This automobile service station was probably built in the 1910s. It was owned and operated by Louis S. Featherstone, but in 1922 Bartell Todd purchased it. This 1929 photograph shows employees posing with delivery trucks in the background at 309 West Main Street. The only person identified is Joe Angelastro, fifth from the left. The service station has been gone for many years, and now the site is part of Visalia's thriving retail district.

STRICTLY BUSINESS

The Visalia Planing Mill traces its beginning to 1894 when Burton U. Heberling and D. M. Toothacre formed a partnership and created a carpentry and construction business on Main Street. The company moved to this new location on the southeast corner of Center and East (now Santa Fe) Streets in 1896, until they moved back to Main Street in 1937. Heberling is second from the left in this 1911 photograph. Today a restaurant occupies the site.

For many years, Robert P. Grant, shown on the right, owned and operated one of Visalia's first bakeries at 211 East Main Street. Grant came to Visalia in 1872 and was a businessman his entire life. He died in 1912, leaving the bakery to his son Austin. Probably constructed in the 1880s, this old building is gone and the area is filled with shops and stores. Coincidentally, one is a bakery.

John R. Coats started his foundry business at Locust and Center Streets around 1886. The business moved several times before Coats set up this shop on Santa Fe Avenue, adjacent to Mill Creek, in 1895. In 1900, Coats sold this building to Burton U. Heberling, his business neighbor who owned the planing mill, and moved his foundry to Main Street. The site is now a parking lot for a restaurant.

In 1892, L. C. Locey established a mortuary business in Visalia. Joshua M. Hadley bought the business located on Court Street in 1919, and in 1923 the Hadley Funeral Chapel moved to its new location at 410 West Center Street. Hadley's son Dud took over the business in 1948. Dud and his wife, Maxine, sold the funeral chapel in 1980. In 2008, the building was remodeled, and it is now a bank and office space.

In 1888, Jasper Harrell had plans prepared for a new three-story building at the southeast corner of Court and Main Streets. When it was finished, the building had a bank on the ground level with upper floors being office and retail space. In 1962, a fire started on the third floor and damaged the building so badly that the second and third floors had to be removed. Today only the ground floor remains, which continues to house a banking concern.

The Automobile Club of Southern California opened its first office in Visalia in 1916. The office moved several times before it opened at this new location at 520 West Mineral King Avenue in December 1941. For 20 years, the auto club remained here before moving again. The old AAA building was used for medical offices, and in 2004, it was moved to another Visalia location to make way for this multistory medical facility.

Built in 1923 at 128 East Main Street, the Bank of Italy building had five stories plus a basement. R. F. Felchlin, a Fresno construction company, supplied the architectural, engineering, and contracting services. The ground level was designed to be a bank, and the other space was set aside for offices. Later it became the Bank of America. Today the ground floor continues to be a bank, and the upper floors still provide office space.

Built in about 1903 on the northeast corner of Main and Garden Streets, this Spanish-style hotel, called the Harvey House, contained shops on the ground floor and rooms for rent on the second story. In 1971, the building was demolished as part of a continuing redevelopment project to make way for a new car lot. The automobile dealership is gone, and the corner is now used as a parking lot.

STRICTLY BUSINESS

The old brick Cohn Building reportedly was constructed in 1857 on the southwest corner of Main and Court Streets. The second floor of the building contained the *Visalia Delta* newspaper and their printing office, while the ground floor contained retail space. Poorly constructed, it was torn down in 1903 and a bank building was constructed in its place. It is possible that the building on the site today is at least part of the old bank structure.

In 1906, Robert "Bert" Cross and a partner constructed the Cross-Horlock Company Hardware building at 116 East Main Street. In 1913, Cross sold his business to Arthur E. Horlock; the new owner continued to use the Cross name on the business. The adjacent Togni Branch stationery store eventually took over the building. The Togni Branch business closed in 2007, and the building is now vacant.

Joseph Hammer owned the Wieland Beer Depot, located on Stevenson Street just north of Oak Street. It had been a brewery site even before Hammer took it over in 1895. This Austrian or German native came to Visalia in 1887 and was well respected for his skill as a brewer. About 1899, Hammer developed inflammatory rheumatism, and he died in 1903. These buildings are gone, and a parking lot exists there today.

The St. Charles Building was constructed in the late 1850s on Court Street, just south of Main Street on the west side of the block. Structurally defective, the building collapsed in 1861 but was rebuilt on the same site shortly thereafter. The rebuilt structure, shown here, included a saloon, billiards parlor, and a music hall. About 1905, the building was torn down, probably due to fire damage. A bank building was constructed on the site, which now houses retail businesses.

This 1903 photograph shows the Visalia Manufacturing Company ice plant and the city water tower, located in the 500 block of East Main Street on the north side. The man at the far right is unidentified, but in the front of the building from left to right are W. J. Hirni, S. J. Scott, George Fickle, and Bob Watson, all employees of the Visalia Manufacturing Company. The buildings shown are gone, and the area is now part of the eastward expanding business district.

The Tulare County Abstract Company, as shown here in this 1939 photograph, was built at 204 West Main Street around 1908. On the far left, the Montgomery Ward building can be seen under construction. Today a coin shop occupies the Tulare County Abstract Company building. Sometime after this photograph was taken, a vintage street clock was relocated here from another Main Street location.

STRICTLY BUSINESS

Believed to have been constructed about 1900, the Balconies Apartments building is on the southwest corner of Garden and Main Streets. The two-story building had retail stores on the ground level and apartments on the second floor. In 1946, the Rountree-Morris Furniture store occupied the building when the first Visalia police officer, Charles Garrison, was killed in the alley behind it. The building still stands, but Garden Street has been blocked off between Main and Acequia Streets, creating Garden Street Plaza.

The *Tulare County Times* newspaper moved into this building on the ground floor in 1903. The structure still stands and is called Times Place. On this site, but not in this building, was the home of another newspaper called the *Equal Rights* *Expositor*. In 1863, at the height of the Civil War, loyal Union soldiers stationed at Visalia's Camp Babbitt destroyed the newspaper office because of its support for the Confederacy.

CHAPTER 5

DIGNIFIED DWELLINGS
AND PUBLIC SERVICE

Built about 1915, the Dudley House stands at the corner of Giddings and Main Streets. The stately home took on the name of the original owners, Benjamin and Helen Dudley, who lived there many years. In 1949, they sold it to two doctors, who in turn sold it to the Methodist Church 10 years later. It became known as Wesley Hall. In 1991, local businessman Frank Cavale bought the building and restored it. It is again the Dudley House.

In 1869, the Visalia Fire Department was organized. David R. Douglass, a local businessman, donated a lot on the southeast corner of Church and Acequia Streets for a firehouse. In 1872, the single-story brick structure was built and a second story added in 1876. This horse-drawn fire engine was purchased in 1869 and remains with the Visalia Fire Department today. The building was demolished in 1909. The site is now the location of the Visalia Convention Center.

DIGNIFIED DWELLINGS AND PUBLIC SERVICE

In 1920, freshman students, obviously in good spirits, parade in front of the Visalia High School on West Main Street, near Conyer Street. A horse is pulling a disabled automobile, and the sign asks, "Where is the VHS Auto Shop?" The Visalia High School building shown here was constructed in 1912 after the original burned to the ground in 1911. It is now the campus of Redwood High School.

Dignified Dwellings and Public Service

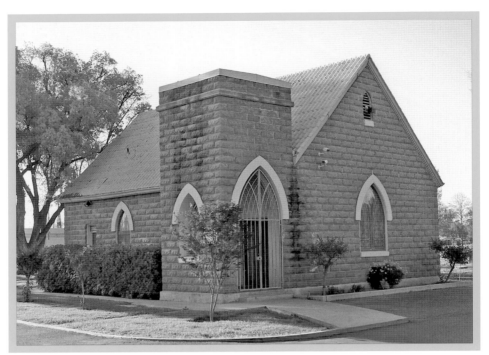

The Visalia Cemetery Chapel was built in 1911 for $3,000. This Gothic Revival block building with beautiful stained-glass windows was a joint project between the Ladies Improvement Society and the City of Visalia. By 1980, the building had fallen into serious disrepair, and its future was in question. Historic preservation groups and individuals rallied to restore it to its original glory. The beautiful chapel stands today as a cemetery focal point.

DIGNIFIED DWELLINGS AND PUBLIC SERVICE

William R. Bowen and his wife, Jessie, lived in this house at 121 North Cottonwood Street in the early 1900s. They owned the Palace Livery Stable located nearby. Shown in this *c.* 1906 photograph are the children, from left to right, William, Inella, Ted, and Laura, with their mother Jessie. Cottonwood Street later changed its name to Encina Street, and today the home site is in Visalia's downtown retail district.

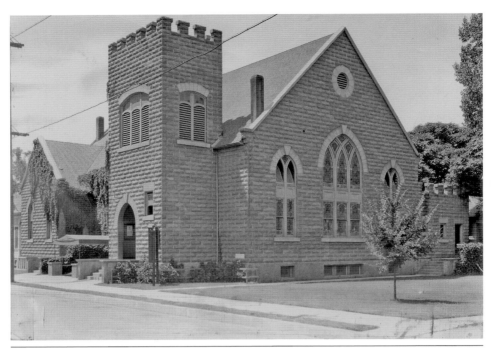

This First Presbyterian Church was built in 1912 at a cost of about $10,000. George Noble, the general contractor, made all the concrete blocks that were used in the church walls and foundation. Located on the southwest corner of Oak and Locust Streets, this church stood until the First Presbyterian Church that stands there today replaced it in 1958. The main entrance to the current church is on Oak Street.

DIGNIFIED DWELLINGS AND PUBLIC SERVICE

Built about 1902 by Herbert Askin, this house was purchased by Samuel C. Brown as a wedding gift for his daughter Maude, who married Dr. James Ennis Combs, a longtime Visalia dentist. In 1984, the house, located on the northwest corner of School and Floral Streets, was purchased and remodeled by attorneys Russ Hurley and Phil Laird and is currently their law office. In this photograph, Mrs. Combs is believed to be sitting on the left holding the child.

After two previous Tulare County hospitals burned to the ground, the county built this brick structure in 1894 for $6,000. The hospital building was the main structure in the complex that occupied the entire block bounded by Murray, Santa Fe, Race, and Bridge Streets. B. G. McDougal and Son of Bakersfield was the architect, and Frank Sharp of Hanford did the construction. The building in this 1910 photograph is gone, but the site continues to provide care for those in need.

DIGNIFIED DWELLINGS AND PUBLIC SERVICE

This Tulare County Jail building was constructed in 1918 on the northeast corner of Oak and Church Streets, the same location as the previous county jail. It served as the county jail until 1962, when a new one was built on another site. The overhead lines for the Visalia Electric Railroad can be seen above the building. Since it was vacated as a jail, the building has been home to offices, art galleries, and restaurants.

Visalia fireman Jude Stringley proudly shows off the ornate Visalia Fire Department Eureka Company hose wagon at the intersection of Acequia and Church Streets. Taken from the Visalia Fire Station, this *c.* 1905 photograph is looking north on Church Street. Visalia's volunteer fire company was organized in 1869. The area on Church Street housed retail stores and continues to do so today.

DIGNIFIED DWELLINGS AND PUBLIC SERVICE

The Brooks Funeral Chapel owned the horse-drawn hearse shown here in 1903. Walter W. Collins, who later became Tulare County sheriff, drove this funeral coach. The Tulare County Courthouse annex building is in the background on the left, and the Masonic Hall is on the right. Both of these buildings are gone. Today the structure on the left is the vacant 1935 annex building.

DIGNIFIED DWELLINGS AND PUBLIC SERVICE

The First Baptist Church in Visalia traces its beginnings to 1869. The faithful met in various places until 1910, when this church was built at the corner of Garden and Mineral King Streets. C. M. Northrup was the pastor at the time of this photograph. Today Garden Street between Main Street and Mineral King Avenue has been abandoned as a street to allow for the building of a large parking structure and the Visalia Convention Center.

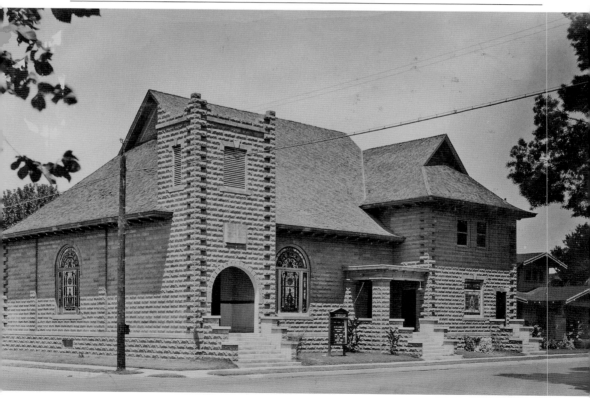

DIGNIFIED DWELLINGS AND PUBLIC SERVICE

Albert Ellis Brooks owned the Brooks Funeral Chapel, located on the southwest corner of Church and School Streets. He began undertaking in Visalia in 1903 and moved here around 1924. After his father died in 1935, Roy Brooks took over the family business and remained at this location until about 1955. In 1875, the funeral chapel building was home to superior court judge Wheaton Gray; it was later sold to the Cutler family. Today it is a labor temple.

The Tulare County traffic squad began in 1916 and eventually became part of the California Highway Patrol. In this photograph taken about 1926, the motorcycle officers pose in front of Wilson Cyclery at 426 East Main Street. From left to right are Luther W. Hogan; Art Benson; Emery L. Dawson; Wayne Wilson, proprietor; Harold Hicks (officer, Visalia Police Department); Leroy Van Gorden; and William "Squeak" Riley. Today the area lies in the path of the downtown expansion to the east.

DIGNIFIED DWELLINGS AND PUBLIC SERVICE

Webster Grammar School, located on Northwest Third Avenue near Pearl Street, opened in 1917 with Carrie Barnett as the first principal. The building was declared unsafe as a school in 1950 and converted into a maintenance shop and storage building. In 1961, fire damaged the structure beyond repair. Only the brick walls remained after the fire, with almost the entire interior destroyed, including its contents. The site is now a Visalia Police Department substation.

In this 1906 photograph, Visalia fireman Jack Sanders is posing near 218 West Grove Street, a home owned by Minnie Abbott Hamilton. He is driving the Visalia Fire Department Chemical No. 1 wagon, pulled by a specially trained team of horses. The Visalia Fire Department was organized in 1869. The Hamilton home remains today on the far left, but another house has been built adjacent to it.

DIGNIFIED DWELLINGS AND PUBLIC SERVICE

For about 75 years, the Tulare County Courthouse with the fancy cupola served the people of Tulare County. It was built in Courthouse Square in 1876 on Court Street, between Oak and Center Streets. In 1935, with help from the Works Progress Administration, an annex courthouse was built adjacent to the old one, connecting the two. The old courthouse building was damaged by an earthquake in 1952 and demolished in the early 1960s. The annex continues to stand today.

The Tulare County traffic squad proudly poses on Center Street, just east of Church Street, about 1930. About this time, it was incorporated into the newly formed California Highway Patrol. The one-story building in the background was the squad's Tulare County Traffic Department office. It was a brick structure built about 1860. From left to right are William "Squeak" Riley, Arthur Thurman, Mike Grady, Leroy Van Gorden, Diamond Phillips, and H. E. Martin. Today the site is a parking lot.

Dignified Dwellings and Public Service

In 1910, the city hall and fire department building was located on the east side of Church Street, between Acequia Street and Mineral King Avenue. The building shown here was demolished to make way for the convention center in 1972. At that time, Church Street was abandoned between Acequia Street and Mineral King Avenue. The old building site is now the convention center courtyard. The original dedication marker from the old building is mounted on the outside wall of the convention center.

The Municipal Auditorium was built on the north side of Acequia Street, between Garden and Bridge Streets, in 1916. It hosted stage plays, political rallies, wrestling matches, National Guard exercises, and many other community events. Both the Visalia and the Tulare County Board of Trade occupied space there. In 1963, the building was found unsafe, and it was torn down. Now a parking structure occupies the site.

DIGNIFIED DWELLINGS AND PUBLIC SERVICE

The idea to build a Tulare County Museum first surfaced in the 1920s, but it took many years for the idea to become a reality. In 1948, the county used $5,000 that Hugh M. Mooney had bequeathed to them and built a museum. The building was small, but it was designed for later additions. The Tulare County Museum, located in historic Mooney Grove Park, opened officially to the public in April 1950.

In December 1898, Emil Seligman and Elwood "E.O." Larkins began constructing their brick building on Church Street between Main and Center Streets. On January 6, 1899, while under construction, the building collapsed and killed a worker named Harvey Hughes. The partnership hired a new contractor to finish the project. Identified on the top of the building are the names Seligman and Larkins. This old office and retail building was demolished in 1967 to make way for a parking lot.

DIGNIFIED DWELLINGS AND PUBLIC SERVICE

The library was a joint construction project between the City of Visalia and the federal government's Works Progress Administration and was dedicated on August 28, 1936. On January 22, 1962, Visalia received 2 inches of snow that covered the library grounds and was just enough to require shoveling of the walkway. This building was vacated and used for storage after the new library was constructed in 1976. In 2008, the WPA building was restored and became the Visalia Children's Library.

www.arcadiapublishing.com

Discover books about the town where you grew up, the cities where your friends and families live, the town where your parents met, or even that retirement spot you've been dreaming about. Our Web site provides history lovers with exclusive deals, advanced notification about new titles, e-mail alerts of author events, and much more.

MADE IN THE USA

Arcadia Publishing, the leading local history publisher in the United States, is committed to making history accessible and meaningful through publishing books that celebrate and preserve the heritage of America's people and places. Consistent with our mission to preserve history on a local level, this book was printed in South Carolina on American-made paper and manufactured entirely in the United States.

This book carries the accredited Forest Stewardship Council (FSC) label and is printed on 100 percent FSC-certified paper. Products carrying the FSC label are independently certified to assure consumers that they come from forests that are managed to meet the social, economic, and ecological needs of present and future generations.

FSC
Mixed Sources
Product group from well-managed forests and other controlled sources

Cert no. SW-COC-001530
www.fsc.org
© 1996 Forest Stewardship Council

Find Your Place in History.